16 EASY CLASSICAL SONGS FOR SOLO VIOLIN

BY ALICIA ENSTROM

ISBN: 9798857901182

HOW TO GET THE AUDIO

The audio files for this book are available for free as downloads or streaming on *troynelsonmusic.com*.

We are available to help you with your audio downloads and any other questions you may have. Simply email *help@troynelsonmusic.com*.

See below for the recommended ways to listen to the audio:

Download Audio Files	Stream Audio Files
• Download Audio Files (Zipped)	• Recommended for CELL PHONES & TABLETS
• Recommended for COMPUTERS on WiFi	• Bookmark this page
• A ZIP file will automatically download to the default "downloads" folder on your computer	• Simply tap the PLAY button on the track you want to listen to
• Recommended: download to a desktop/laptop computer *first*, then transfer to a tablet or cell phone	• Files also available for streaming or download at *soundcloud.com/troynelsonbooks*
• Phones & tablets may need an "unzipping" app such as iZip, Unrar or Winzip	
• Download on WiFi for faster download speeds	

To download the companion audio files for this book, visit: troynelsonmusic.com/audio-downloads/

INTRODUCTION

I love music of all genres and have always enjoyed learning tunes or pieces within these various styles. To me, music—classical, jazz, fiddle, pop, hip-hop, etc.—are simply colors or different languages within a universal vocabulary. Learning and playing tunes within all of these styles enables you to expand your coloring box of skills and musical communication in every direction!

I grew up classically trained and fell in love with many of the classical art world standards and how they transcend time. The classical pieces found in this book translate so well to the violin and should be somewhat familiar. Each tune features two arrangements, one easy version for beginners and one intermediate version. The intermediate version is simply a variation of the beginner-level arrangement.

Every song is also written in both standard notation (i.e., traditional notes on a page) and tablature, or "tab," which will help you understand finger placement on your instrument. You can read more about both in the Notes and Tab Primer (page 5).

You may also want to add a bit of *vibrato*, which is a rapid fluctuation in the pitch of a note. Vibrato really helps notes sing! However, before you start to add vibrato, I think it's important to make sure the songs have beautiful pitch and intonation—without the wiggles. Once you feel locked in on the tune, you can then begin to add vibrato and make it sing further! You can learn more about this technique in Vibrato for Beginners (page 4).

The violin is a really cool instrument, one that tends to lean mostly towards the human voice. I hope you enjoy learning the violin more intimately while using some of my favorite classical melodies!

VIBRATO FOR BEGINNERS

Vibrato is one of those things that every beginning violin student has asked me about, whether they're five years old or 70! It's such a lovely sound if done correctly and is a really fun tool to have in your violin toolbox. Vibrato is a process, so don't feel like you need to rush it. Take your time and practice frequently in front of a mirror. OK, let's begin…

First of all, be sure that your left hand is in proper position with your wrist down, leading straight into your forearm, and not pushing upward or propping your violin up. Next, be sure that you have a little window of space between your thumb and index finger right under the violin neck. This is important, as it allows room for the hand to move. Also, keep all four left-hand fingers above the fingerboard, not tucked under it. This will help to keep your hand relaxed, as well as just being good form overall!

The only touchpoints on the violin neck during vibrato should be your thumb and the finger(s) you are using to play the note(s). These touchpoints act as a "hinge" for your hand to swing back and forth on.

As your hand "swings" back and forth, your finger will roll back (flat pitch) so you can see your fingertip, then roll back up to pitch, and then back down and up, etc. You get the idea.

There's a lot more to vibrato but this will get you started. Incidentally, you might want to start with your second or third finger. I've found those fingers to be the easiest for beginners to relax and move correctly.

Also, be sure that you're not holding your violin up by your left hand; instead, hold it with your shoulder and chin. Your hand needs a steady place to move easily on, without having to hold up the violin, too.

OK, that should get you going on vibrato!

NOTES AND TAB PRIMER

There are a few things to know in regard to reading the music in this book. Not many violin books use tablature, or tab, but this one uses both standard notation and violin tab, so you can choose which suits you best—or use both!

In this section, you'll learn how to read notes in both standard notation and tab, and how to count basic rhythms (which are consistent in both formats). (**Note:** If you feel overwhelmed while reading this section, don't let that stop you. Instead, try to keep moving forward and just refer back to this section whenever you have a question about one of these topics as you go through the book.)

NOTES

Traditional music notation is written on a staff consisting of five lines and four spaces. Several different clefs exist in music, but violin music is written on the treble clef.

Each line and space of the staff represents a pitch. The five lines of the treble clef, from bottom to top, are: E–G–B–D–F (mnemonically: "Every Good Boy Does Fine"). The four spaces, from bottom to top, are: F–A–C–E ("FACE").

The musical alphabet is a series of letters used to identify pitch. Unlike the English alphabet, which consists of 26 letters, the musical alphabet is limited to just the first seven letters:

A B C D E F G

Each pitch in music is assigned a letter name, and these letter names correspond to a line or space on the staff. The lower the pitch, the lower its position on the staff; the higher the pitch, the higher its position. When a pitch is lower than the lowest pitch of the staff, or when a pitch is higher than the highest pitch on the staff, ledger lines are used (two exceptions are the D note that directly precedes the first line of the staff, and the G note that immediately follows the last line of the staff).

Below is a music staff containing the notes (and their names) found in first position on the violin, as well as a fingerboard diagram indicating where these note are played and which fingers play them. All notes are natural, not sharp (half step higher) or flat (half step lower), in this example.

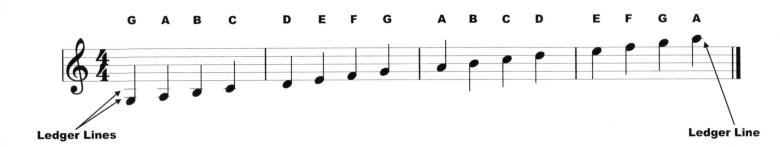

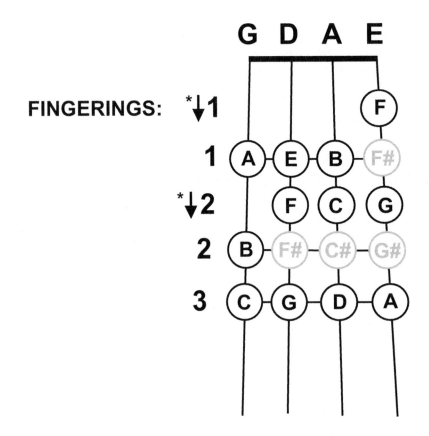

*indicates lowered fingering

In traditional Western music (the music we listen to and play), natural half steps occur between B and C, and E and F. When we need to raise or lower a pitch a half step—the pitches found in between the other notes of the musical alphabet—we simply add a sharp symbol (♯) or flat symbol (♭) before the notehead, respectively. To cancel out a sharp or flat and return the note to its unaltered pitch, we add a natural sign, as shown below.

TAB

In tab, there are four lines, one for each string of the violin. The lowest/thickest string on the violin (G) is also the lowest string on the tab staff. The numbers tell you which fingers to use, and the lines tell you what strings to place those fingers on.

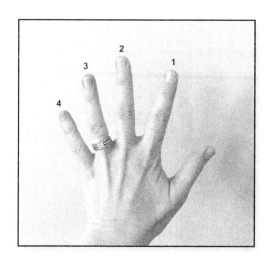

1 = index finger

2 = middle finger

3 = ring finger

4 = pinky finger

Here is how the violin's first-position notes look in tab:

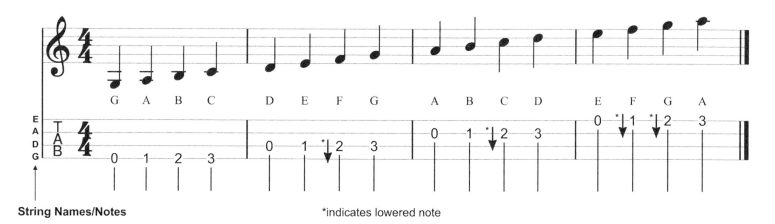

String Names/Notes   *indicates lowered note

In tab, a downward-pointing arrow next to a fingering number indicates that the finger is to be played a half step lower than its basic fingering position. For example, on the E string in the previous example, an arrow precedes the numbers 1 and 2, meaning those two notes, F and G, are played a half step lower than the notes that the index (1) and middle (2) fingers play in basic first position, F♯ and G♯.

From the open string, basic first position is one whole step to the 1st finger (a whole step is about an inch on a 4/4 [full-sized] violin), a whole step from the 1st to the 2nd finger, a half step from the 2nd to the 3rd finger (a half step is about a half inch), and another whole step from the 3rd to the 4th finger.

For reference, here are all of the notes in basic first position on the fingerboard, as well as the fingers that play them. As illustrated below, High 3 fingering is a half-step higher than the regular 3rd-finger position.

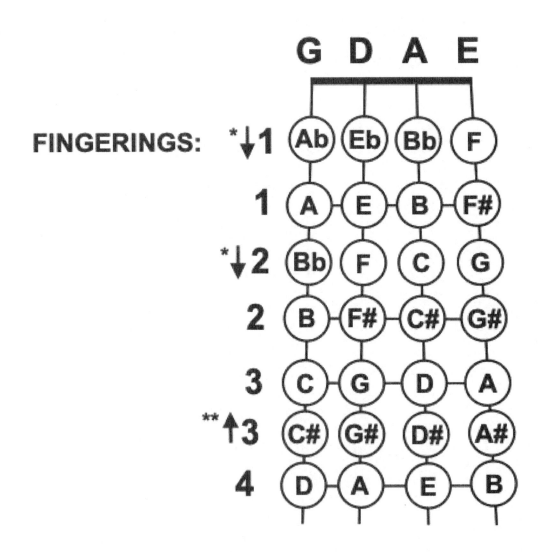

FINGERINGS:

*indicates lowered fingering
**indicates raised fingering

AUTUMN
Performance Notes

Antonio Vivaldi's "Autumn" is in the key of F major, with one flat, B♭. The notes of the F major scale are: F–G–A–B♭–C–D–E

THREE TIPS FOR PLAYING "AUTUMN"

1. There are several instances where double upbows are used. A double upbow is a little different from a slur in that the bow will continue in the direction in which it has been traveling, but there will be a small space between the notes. For examples of the double upbow, look at and listen to the opening measures.

2. The fun thing about this tune is that there are absolutely no accidentals! The only notes that you will use in this melody are those that you practiced in the F major scale.

3. In the intermediate version, the melody has been altered a bit and requires your bow to switch quickly between the A and D strings. Check out the first four measures of each version and notice the differences in notes and bow-feel.

EASY VERSION

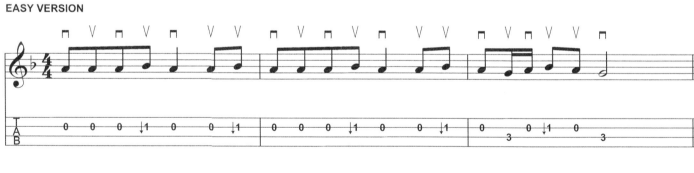

INTERMEDIATE VERSION

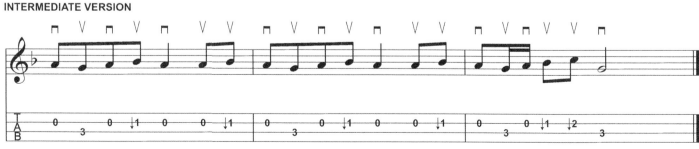

AUTUMN
Easy Version

AUTUMN
Intermediate Version

AVÉ MARIA
Performance Notes

Written by Franz Schubert, this arrangement of "Avé Maria" is written in the key of C major, which has no sharps or flats and is a very happy key for the violin!

The notes of the C major scale are: C–D–E–F–G–A–B. Below is the C major scale for you to practice.

THREE TIPS FOR PLAYING "AVÉ MARIA"

1. There are quite a few accidentals. An accidental is a note that isn't part of the original key signature. Look through the tune and notice any additionally marked sharps, flats, or naturals. Some of these accidentals result in very squishy fingerings (as I like to call them), meaning the fingers will be very close to one another on the fingerboard.

2. Rhythmically, "Avé Maria" incorporates quicker notes, or 16th notes. You'll notice these 16ths in bars 4 and 6. Take note when listening to the accompanying audio track.

3. This song also utilizes 8th-note triplets, as shown in bars 8–11 and bars 15–20. It's important to not only play this rhythm correctly, but to watch your bow and string crossings. If that's not enough, don't forget those accidentals that show themselves in these passages.

BARS 8–11, EASY VERSION

BARS 15–20, EASY VERSION

Once you get this down, it's smooth sailing!

AVÉ MARIA
Easy Version

AVÉ MARIA
Intermediate Version

CANON IN D
Perfomance Notes

Written by Johann Pachelbel, "Canon in D" is in the key of, well... D major! D major has two sharps, F♯ and C♯. The notes of the D major scale are: D–E–F♯–G–A–B–C♯

THREE TIPS FOR PLAYING "CANON IN D"

1. I'm sure you will recognize this tune! Nonetheless, be sure to listen to the accompanying audio track to hear this version. Also be sure to notice that, over the course of the arrangement, the melodic variations move from half notes to quarter notes and then to 8th notes before moving back to half notes.

2. The intermediate version simply adds melodic phrases and ornamentations, building on the beginner version.

3. Really let those half notes sing as you change notes—feel the connectivity!

CANON IN D
Easy Version

CANON IN D
Intermediate Version

CLAIR DE LUNE
Performance Notes

Claude Debussy's Clair de Lune is arranged here in the key of A major, with three sharps, F♯, C♯, and G♯.

The notes in the A major scale are: A–B–C♯–D–E–F♯–G♯

THREE TIPS FOR PLAYING "CLAIR DE LUNE"

1. You will notice quite a few slurs in this piece, as well as many ties that go across the bar lines. A *tie* simply "ties" two note values of the same pitch into one longer note. For practice, take the first five measures of the piece and really watch your bow as you tackle the rhythm! Be sure to listen to the practice track to hear them, as well.

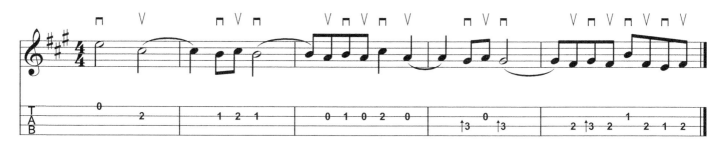

2. Once you feel really secure in the rhythm of this piece, try to really make it sing with long, connected bows! And watch out for that G♯ on the G string—a squishy first finger, or Low 1, right at the start of the fingerboard!

3. The intermediate version includes some additional melodic material, so take a peek and see where that happens.

CLAIR DE LUNE
Easy Version

CLAIR DE LUNE
Intermediate Version

FÜR ELISE
Performance Notes

Beethoven's "Für Elise" is arranged here in the key of G minor, with two flats, B♭ and E♭. G minor is the relative minor of B♭ major. A *relative key* means that the two scales share the same notes (as well as the same key signature) but they begin on different notes, making one major and one minor.

The notes of the G minor scale are: G–A–B♭–C–D–E♭–F

(For reference, the notes of the B♭ major scale are: B♭–C–D–E♭–F–G–A)

THREE TIPS FOR PLAYING "FÜR ELISE"

1. There are a few tricky accidentals in this tune. Look through the song and notice any additionally marked sharps and naturals. In particular, the main melody has two accidentals on the same note—the note C is played as C♯ but then returns to C natural, which is part of the G minor scale.

2. Two downbows separated by an apostrophe (') does not mean you should replace the bow at the frog. Instead, think of it as a breath—stopping the bow where it is on its journey and, if you need more bow, placing it near the middle of the stick.

3. In the intermediate version, be mindful of the slurs and change in bowing direction, as well as the additional note in bar 4.

FÜR ELISE
Easy Version

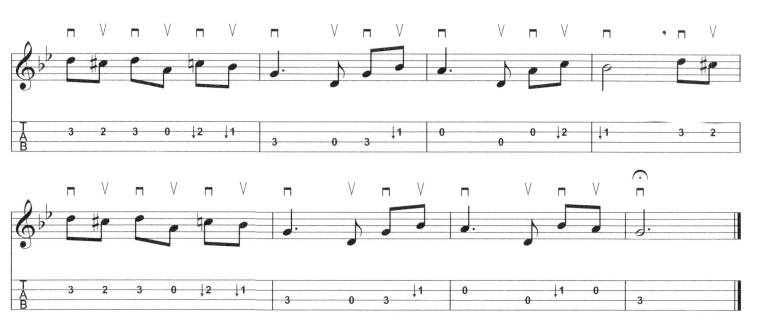

FÜR ELISE
Intermediate Version

GAVOTTE
Performance Notes

"Gavotte," by French composer François-Joseph Gossec, is arranged here in the key of G major, with one sharp, F♯. G major is one of the friendliest violin keys—or at least I think so!

The notes of the G major scale are: G–A–B–C–D–E–F♯

THREE TIPS FOR PLAYING "GAVOTTE"

1. There are only a few accidentals in the easy version of this tune. Look throughout the arrangement to see where they pop up. They're sharps, so you'll be raising your finger position.

2. With a quick glance, you'll notice apostrophes and consecutive downbows every two bars. While this doesn't denote restarting your bow from the very bottom, it will require a little choreography (practice!). At the end of each two-bar pattern, slightly lift the bow from the string before placing the center of the bow back onto the string for the start of the next note.

3. The intermediate version rearranges the order of the 8th notes. Can you see the differences between the two melodies?

GAVOTTE
Easy Version

GAVOTTE
Intermediate Version

JESU, JOY OF MAN'S DESIRING
Performance Notes

Bach's "Jesu, Joy of Man's Desiring" is arranged here in the key of G major, with one sharp, F♯. The notes of the G major scale are: G–A–B–C–D–E–F♯

THREE TIPS FOR PLAYING "JESU"

1. There are no accidentals, so the notes you practice in the scale are the notes you will use in the song. However, for the most part, this piece changes bows on every note. Can you make connections between the notes so you don't hear every bow change? Try to connect the bow changes smoothly and continue the tone even as the bow changes direction and your fingers change notes.

2. The intermediate version has some new rhythms, so be sure to take note.

3. In both versions, you can practice using your 4th finger as opposed to open strings for a variation in sound. Anywhere there is a "0" in the tab, you can replace that note with a 4th finger on the previous string for a slightly different sound. For example, a "0" on the A string is an A note that can also be played with a "4" on the D string. Notice how it sounds and feels. Which sounds better to you? Which is physically easier? And which do you prefer overall?

JESU, JOY OF MAN'S DESIRING
Easy Version

JESU, JOY OF MAN'S DESIRING
Intermediate Version

LARGO
Performance Notes

"Largo," by George Frideric Handel, is arranged here in the key of G major (one of our favorite scales!), with one sharp, F♯. The notes of the G major scale are: G–A–B C–D–E–F♯

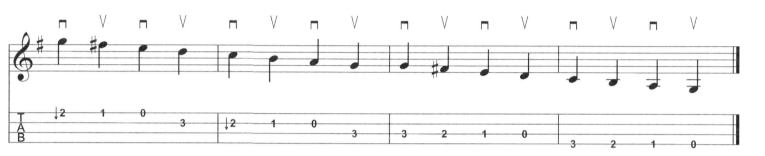

THREE TIPS FOR PLAYING "LARGO"

1. There are a few accidentals in the easy version of this tune. Take a peek and make sure they don't surprise you!

2. You will see various rhythms in this version, as well. There are both triplets and notes tied together (see "Clair de Lune" for the definition of a "tie" if you're unfamiliar). On notes tied across the bar (as in the very first bar), simply hold the note for its full rhythmic value—that is, the original note's value plus the value of the tied note. Do not reemphasize the note on beat 1 of the next bar (bar 2).

3. In the intermediate version, you will see more rhythmic changes, as well as some additional melodic material. Navigate to where rhythms differ from the beginner version and practice these spots (see below).

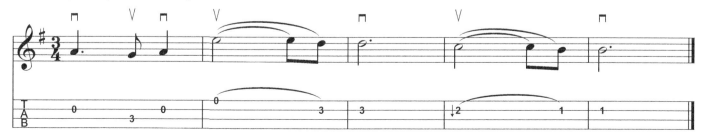

LARGO
Easy Version

LARGO
Intermediate Version

45

LULLABY
Performance Notes

"Lullaby," by German composer Johannes Brahms, is arranged here in the key of F major, with one flat, B♭.

The notes of the F major scale are: F–G–A–B♭–C–D–E

THREE TIPS FOR PLAYING "LULLABY"

1. There are no accidentals in this tune, so prepare by practicing the scale above and never stray from those notes.

2. You probably know this tune quite well. When playing, try to really make the piece sing with mellow and subtle bow changes that are smooth and not aggressive.

3. The intermediate version has some rhythmic variations (see bars 1 and 3, for example). Spot the differences before you begin.

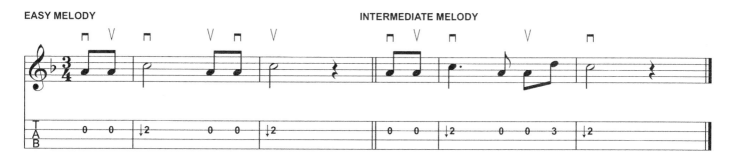

LULLABY
Easy Version

LULLABY
Intermediate Version

MINUET IN G
Performance Notes

The key of "Minuet in G" is right there in its title—G major! The key of G major has one sharp, F♯.

The notes in the G major scale are: G–A–B–C–D–E–F♯

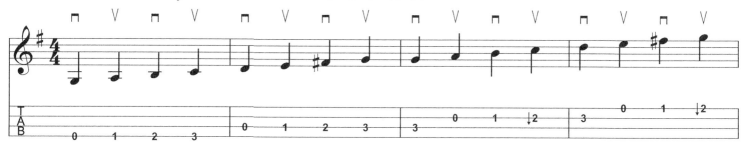

THREE TIPS FOR PLAYING "MINUET IN G"

1. There is only one accidental in this arrangement, C♯, and it occurs in the B section. Keep your eyes and ears open for all areas where this happens!

2. There are double upbows in some of the phrasing, starting in measure 2. This bowing pattern is prevalent throughout this piece. Unlike some other slower songs, you can add a little space between these upbows. This piece is much more dynamic and not as quietly sweet!

3. The intermediate version features some note variations and thus string crossings for the double upbows (see measures 2 and 4). Be sure to practice the necessary choreography for these string-crossing double upbows!

BARS 1–4, INTERMEDIATE VERSION

MINUET IN G
Easy Version

MINUET IN G
Intermediate Version

NOCTURNE
Performance Notes

This arrangement of Frédéric Chopin's "Nocturne" is in the key of D major, with two sharps, F♯ and C♯. This key is another one of my favorites and a happy key for the violin!

The notes in the D major scale are: D–E–F♯–G–A–B–C♯

THREE TIPS FOR PLAYING "NOCTURNE"

1. Accidentals, accidentals, accidentals! Locate all those measures with new friends and take time to make a plan and see how the notes physically work with your fingers. Even if you are mostly using the standard notation, the tabs might come in handy here so you can see both the fingerings and the notes.

2. This tune is in 3/4 time, which means there are three beats to every measure—a waltz!

3. In addition to more accidentals, you will notice quite a few slurs in the intermediate version. Since this is a very calm, beautiful tune, strive for fluid connectivity from your bow and bow arm to the strings as you change pitches under those slurs. Practice these slurs before tackling the tune in its entirety!

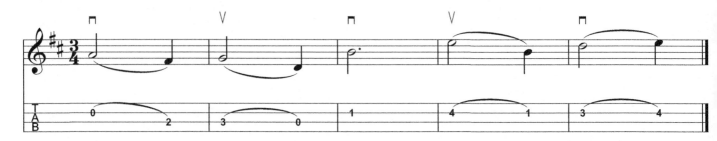

NOCTURNE
Easy Version

NOCTURNE
Intermediate Version

ODE TO JOY
Performance Notes

Beethoven's "Ode to Joy" is arranged here in the key of A major, with three sharps, F#, C#, and G#.

The notes of the A major scale are: A–B–C#–D–E–F#–G#

THREE TIPS FOR PLAYING "ODE TO JOY"

1. There are a few apostrophes in the beginner melody. Simply think of them as a place to restart new melodic material. You don't need to do anything epic with your bow other than stop it and restart the sound!

2. The intermediate version has many additions, including more slurred notes, which will require a little bowing and string-crossing mapping. Bars 1 and 2 are shown below for practice.

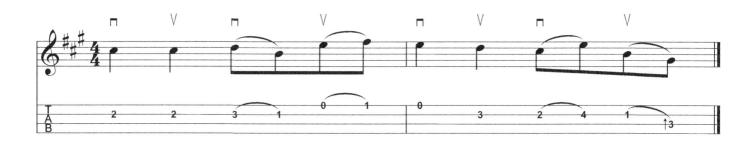

3. Be sure to make all note transitions as smooth as possible in both versions.

ODE TO JOY
Easy Version

ODE TO JOY
Intermediate Version

SPRING
Performance Notes

Vivaldi's "Spring" is in the key of A major, with three sharps, F♯, C♯, and G♯.

The notes of the A major scale are: A–B–C♯–D–E–F♯–G♯

THREE TIPS FOR PLAYING "SPRING"

1. There are no huge surprises in "Spring—just a lot of repeated material, which makes it fairly easy to memorize. However, you can make it sound more interesting by changing dynamics (one time loud, one time softer, etc.) to create variations in sound.

2. The intermediate version has a new rhythm and bow crossing (see bars 2–4 below). Test out your bow choreography!

BARS 2–4, INTERMEDIATE VERSION

3. Similarly, test out the bowing coordination in the second half of the arrangement. Play bars 14–17, shown below, to practice maneuvering back to the E string.

BARS 14–17, INTERMEDIATE VERSION

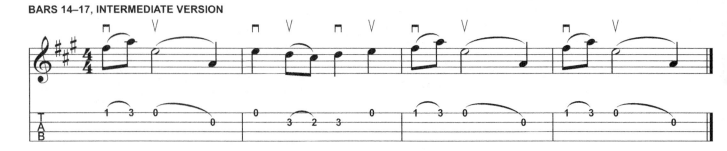

SPRING
Easy Version

SPRING
Intermediate Version

THE BLUE DANUBE
Performance Notes

"The Blue Danube," by Austrian composer Johann Strauss, is brought to you in the key of A major, with three sharps, F♯, C♯, and G♯. It also features three beats per measure… a waltz!

The notes in the A major scale are: A–B–C♯–D–E–F♯–G♯

THREE TIPS FOR PLAYING "THE BLUE DANUBE"

1. The G♯ in this tune will be a bit different—you will be playing a squishy first finger, or Low 1, on your lowest string, G. Look at bars 8 and 9 to see how that differs from your open string.

2. The intermediate version simply takes the melody you just played and adds some additional rhythms.

3. The intermediate version also adds some slurs! Focus on the rhythm-and-bow choreography for this new version.

THE BLUE DANUBE
Easy Version

THE BLUE DANUBE
Intermediate Version

TRÄUMEREI
Performance Notes

German composer Robert Schumann's "Träumerei" is arranged here in the key of F major, with one flat, B♭.

The notes in the F major scale are: F–G–A–B♭–C–D–E

THREE TIPS FOR PLAYING "TRÄUMEREI"

1. There are a few unexpected accidentals in this one. Make sure to take note of them.

2. There is also a fair amount of string crossings during the 8th-note passages. Take a moment to practice your choreography, noting which string your bow will be on or be moving to.

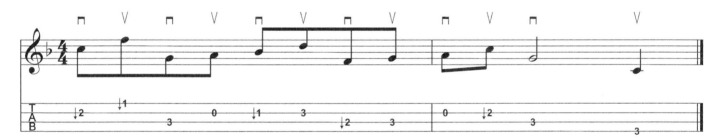

3. The intermediate version takes some of those 8th-note passages you practiced and switches the notes around. Notice the differences and practice the string crossings with the new notes.

TRÄUMEREI
Easy Version

TRÄUMEREI
Intermediate Version

WALTZ OF THE FLOWERS
Performance Notes

Tchaikovsky's "Waltz of the Flowers" is arranged here in D major, with two sharps F# and C#.

The notes of the D major scale are: D–E–F#–G–A–B–C#

THREE TIPS FOR PLAYING "WALTZ OF THE FLOWERS"

1. "Waltz of the Flowers" might be the trickiest tune in this book simply because of the accidentals throughout. Take a moment to locate all of them. You can practice many of them in the following excerpt.

2. Also notice the series of apostrophes that occur. Think of these spots as "breaths" that propel you into the next phrase.

3. Notice in the intermediate version that more notes have been added, rhythmically, and in doing so, even more accidentals. Practice the melody on the next page, paying close attention to fingerings, both squishy (low) and regular.

BARS 13-16, INTERMEDIATE VERSION

BARS 24-32, INTERMEDIATE VERSION

WALTZ OF THE FLOWERS
Easy Version

WALTZ OF THE FLOWERS
Intermediate Version

ABOUT THE AUTHOR

Alicia Enstrom is a classically trained violinist, composer, producer, and reformed circus runaway (Cirque du Soleil and Barrage). Alicia has performed as a soloist on stages throughout the world, for blockbuster movie soundtracks and video games (*Call of Duty*, *Madden NFL*, *The Walking Dead*), with Billboard 100 artists (Willie Nelson, Paul McCartney, Dolly Parton, John Legend), on TV awards shows (Grammys, ACM, CMA, CMT), and with the most recognized symphonies in the world.

Alicia is a unique artist whose work spans classical, orchestral, pop, and ambient electronic music. She has released numerous self-produced projects, which she performs live with looping pedals. In 2018, Alicia won The Ear, a classical composition competition in New York City, and, in 2020, she was a finalist in the Sundance Film Music and Sound Design Lab.

Alicia was nominated for an Academy of Country Music Specialty Instrument Player of the Year Award in 2020 and was the winner of both the International Songwriting Competition and the Unsigned Only Music Competition in the Instrumental Music categories in 2021. She has performed with the Radio City Christmas Spectacular in 2021 and 2022, toured with Kelsea Ballerini in 2022, recorded on Luke Combs' *Gettin' Old* album (2023), and performed with Ed Sheeran on his Mathematics Tour. Alicia's music is released via Tone Tree Music and is available on MusicBed.

Printed in Great Britain
by Amazon

46260010R00046